Lapidary for Beginners

Comprehensive Step By Step Blueprint to Lapidary Processes - Tumbling, Cutting, Cabbing, Carving, and Faceting For Beginners

Introduction

They say the lapidary can develop the splendor of the precious jewel of the mine (Francis Alexander Durivage[1]). One can work on a natural mineral/stone, whether a precious stone, semiprecious stone, or any other mineral crystal, to display its beauty.

Are you wondering how?

The lapidary process brings pure value from a seemingly uninteresting material, making it an art that every lover of beautiful gemstones would want to master.

But,

What is lapidary?

Lapidary involves working with minerals and organic non-mineral materials to make jewelry and other decorative objects. In simple terms, it is the process of dealing with precious stones to turn them into beautiful pieces.

For example, do you know how hard stones become beautiful diamonds, the turquoise stones that produce colorful jewelry, or the priceless soft stone carvings? It's all in the work of lapidary.

Lapidary is an art that has been around since the Stone Age when people used stones to make tools. It has continued to evolve, becoming a much more skilled art requiring precision and creativity. It is a skill that involves cutting, faceting, polishing, engraving, and dealing with gems using the techniques we shall look at in detail in this book.

A person who deals with this work is called a **lapidarist** or **lapidary**. And stones that have not been worked on and are in their raw nature are known as **rough stones**.

So,

Do you want to pursue lapidary as a business, or are you fascinated by the amazing and beautiful things that a lapidarist produces and would like to learn it as a hobby? Well, you are in the right place.

Since you are new to this art area, you probably are wondering...

What do you need to know before you begin?

What tools or equipment do I need to use?

What kind of stones will I be dealing with?

What are the procedures involved?

How long does it take to come up with an object or jewelry, among other things?

This book will give you detailed information on this and much more, and by the time you get to the end, you will be all set to take your lapidary journey to the next level.

So, let's get started!

Table of Contents

Chapter 1: A Brief History of the Lapidary Process

Before learning about this beautiful art, let's first look at how it came to be and all the developments and improvements that different lapidaries have made since discovery.

The term "lapidar" originated from the French word "*lapidaire*" which means "One skilled in working with precious stone" (Online Etymology Dictionary[2]). It is probably one of the most ancient professions inman's history and might continue for many more years.

To begin, let's look at how people practiced ancient lapidary.

The Tools, Stones, and the Process Used in Ancient Lapidary

There had to be tools, stones, and a procedure for making different things from rocks to practice lapidary.

Do you know any of them?

Here they are:

The Tools

During the Stone Age, man hammered tools from stones, probably by hitting one rock on another. Through this process, he discovered that some stones were softer than others and, therefore, more suitable to create markings on them than on the harder ones.

Studies[3] show that the Egyptians used turquoise, Amethyst, and other semiprecious stones, many years ago to make jewelry. The ancient Greeks also used them to make their drinking vessels. The other group of people that used this art were the Indo-Aryans of India between 1-1000 A.D.

The practice continued after the 10th century, showing that it was a continuous practice that kept advancing into the world. The Indians would trade their lapidary items with the Africans and vice versa during this period (Open Edition Journals[4]).

The main tools used during the lapidary process were:

- Drills made out of animal bones.

- Saws made out of reeds.

They shaped and smoothed their work by grinding the softer stones/minerals over harder ones (bruting). All this was made possible by discovering the hardness and softness of rocks.

As early as the Stone Age, man could identify the distinguishing smoothness and polishing effect of stones found in flowing rivers compared to those found in other places. With this emerged the desire to find out what caused this distinct feature. Was it the continuous flow of water on the rocks? Or was it the rubbing of minerals contained in the water with the surface of these rocks?

It is through these observations that man was able to come up with more advanced tools and machinery. It created the need to devise ways of smoothing and polishing stones to create value.

With civilization, the tools used for stone crafting and designing developed. Between the 13th and 15th centuries, lapidaries began to use **hammers** and **chisels** to work on precious stones. They would then polish them with the **chippings and grit** that came off the harder stones during chiseling. Later, they mixed the grit with water to make the polishing process more effective.

Fast forward to the 18th and 19th centuries and beyond:

British inventors created the industrial revolution in the late 18th and early 19th centuries. This invention had significant technological changes that helped lapidaries develop better tools.

The good news is,

The tools used today are much easier to use and more efficient. And what's more fulfilling is that lapidary tools/equipment and techniques development has not stopped.

The Stones

During the Stone Age, man made a discovery that was quite a game-changer in the world of stone crafting that entailed the uniqueness of different stones in terms of their color, texture, and configuration.

For instance, the early miners and stone smiths realized that stone elements have different patterns, some of which were lovely. Through this, they could sort out stones and craft them for various purposes, such as adornment.

Do you know some of the stones that have existed for the longest?

Here they are:

- *The jade*

The jade was first discovered in China and given the name "*yu*" which means "royal ge" ([visualcapitalist.com5](visualcapitalist.com)). It was also found in Japan, Korea, and Southeast Asia.

Initially, people used this stone to make tools, but due to its rarity and beautiful nature, they began to design ornaments, carvings, and other decorative artifacts.

- *Amber*

Amber is another kind of stone discovered in some parts of the Baltic countries (on the shores of the Baltic Sea) as early as the Stone Age period. It is formed out of tree resin and is, therefore, lighter than most types of stones. In addition, this stone has insects, small animals, and plants, which gives it a unique feature.

Amber is found in different colors; mainly brown, orange, yellow, and translucent. Its lightweight nature and beautiful color made it easy to make ornaments and jewelry.

- *Quartz*

Quartz is a crystal-clear precious stone that the Greeks commonly knew in ancient times as "krystallos" or "rock crysta" (Britannica.com[6]). It is transparent/translucent, giving it a unique feature.

There are different kinds of quartz: Rose quartz, Agate, Rock crystal, and Amethyst. Rose quartz is one of the common ancient types, discovered as early as 7000 B.C. in present-day Iraq. In the early years, it was used mainly by the Romans and the Assyrians to make jewelry (gia.edu[7]).

Quartz is now used to make glass, ceramics, and other devices. When crushed, it is used in sandpaper, grindstones, and sandblasting.

- *Glass*

Glass, as an object, was discovered about 2000 B.C. in Iraq. It was also found in parts of Egypt and was mainly used to make glass beads and other jewelry. About 100 B.C., the smiths-men of Alexandria found a way of making dishes using molds. The people of Phoenicia later identified a way of blowing molten glass to create glass vessels.

There was also the discovery of flat glass and tinted glass in Venice, a skill they learned from interacting with the Romans. The glass-making process continued to evolve through the 19th and 20th centuries and is still developing.

- *Turquoise stones*

They date back to 3000 B.C. and are believed to have originated from Egyptian tombs in ancient times and were used to enhance the beauty of ornaments, such as gold necklaces

Later on, people from present-day Iran discovered turquoise stones of high quality. And even though turquoise stones are still used today, due to their rare nature, you will likely find some synthetically modified low-quality turquoise stones.

- *Diamond*

Diamond was first found in India around 400-301 B.C. and was highly valued for its beautiful nature. It was also the hardest known natural mineral, becoming a valuable stone for cutting, grinding, drilling, and engraving tools.

Other stones used in the lapidary process in ancient history included sapphire, ruby, and emerald.

The Process

The lapidary process in ancient times involved two main steps:

- *Cutting*

During the process, the lapidarists would use tools made of hard stones to cut the other stones into smaller pieces depending on their specifications.

- *Polishing*

They would then polish stones by rubbing them severally against fine grits of harder stones such as the diamond, quartz, and emery.

Around the 15th century, lapidarist developed advanced polishing tools. They were made of wheels (also referred to as laps or mills) which were water-powered, applying the concept of smoothened stones found in flowing rivers.

Is this the same process used today?

Even though the cutting and polishing concept from the 1400s is still used during lapidary, technology has made it better and more manageable, as you will find out in the next chapter.

Chapter 2: Modern-day Lapidary Processes

It is interesting to learn that, even though the lapidary process has evolved throughout the years, the techniques used have not changed much. The concept is close to the one used in ancient times, but the tools and equipment used have been advanced to make the work more efficient.

However, the steps are similar to those used in the old times. Do you remember them? Yes, the modern lapidary process entails cutting and polishing, only that they have added buffing and a few more steps to make the stones more appealing.

The main categories of the lapidary process are: cutting, tumbling, cabbing, faceting, and carving

In the following chapters, we shall look at the lapidary processes in detail, i.e., the science behind stone cutting and what it will take for you to gain the experience to produce beautiful artwork from your precious gems.

This chapter will cover the first process; cutting raw stones.

So, let's see what it all entails!

Cutting

As a lapidarist, you will find yourself dealing with different rough stones. Some will be small and others large, with diverse and uneven shapes (unformed).

Before cutting your rough stones, you must study their internal and external characteristics.

 Here is why:

- First, this will help you identify the weak points of your stone and the areas you need to remove to maintain the gem's value.

- It will also help you know and recognize fractures, different color shades, and the hardness or softness of the stone, among other things.

During cutting, you will want to do it so that the end product will be a valuable piece that stands out and displays its unique features. You also want to make maximum use of your rough stone (you do not want to waste most of it in the cutting process).

For this to happen, you first have to learn about the tools used in cutting stones.

So, let's look at the tools you will be using:

Tools Used in Stone Cutting

- ## Rock Hammer

https://www.shutterstock.com/image-vector/illustration-line-art-geological-hammer-260nw-2363913569.jpg

A rock hammer, also known as the geologist's hammer, is a simple tool for cutting stones. It has two heads, one on each side. In some hammers, one head is chiseled while the other is flat and squared, as shown in image 1 above.

The geological hammers with a sharp edge (pick head) instead of the chisel edge are known as the rock pick, prospecting/prospector pick, or geological pick. Image 2 shows a rock pick (see its sharp-pointed edge); the sharp point makes it easier to break harder stones:

Most of these hammers are made of one-piece hardened steel, both the head and handle.

Why?

✓ To ensure they last longer.

✓ To make cutting the hard rocks easier.

However, there are less sturdy and less expensive hammers/picks whose handles are hollow, rounded, and made of wood. These may not work on some types of stones, especially those that are hard.

But what are the uses of this tool?

Here they are:

- *In the field and workshop.*

A geologist uses it in the field to retrieve a new surface on a rock.

As a lapidarist, you will use it in the workshop to break the stones to reveal their internal characteristics. This will enable you to work with the stone in its best form, i.e., it breaks the rough rocks into smaller pieces, ready for the subsequent processes.

- *To determine the stone's hardness or softness*

The rock hammer is used to determine a stone's hardness or softness and texture based on the composition of its mineral grains. Lapidarists gently tapped the stone with the hammer on the different surfaces to determine these features.

- *To break large pieces and remove weak and unwanted materials*

You will use the flat side of the hammer to break large stone pieces into smaller ones.

You will use the chisel-shaped side to remove the soft materials and unwanted sharp edges on the stone. For example, when placing stones inside a heavy bag or box, you might need to cut them to prevent rock chips from flying out and causing damage.

However, if/when breaking stones of different hardness, do it separately to avoid damaging the softer stones.

To break a stone, place the flat side down, then hit it with the hammer until you get the desired size. When done, remember to keep the tiny pieces that come off while cutting, as you will use them to tumble/smoothen your stones (a process that we shall look at next in this book).

A rock hammer does not use much precision, but it is still an essential tool for cutting stones. However, whenever you need to make precision when cutting a rough stone using the rock hammer, you could use a process called **cutting through a kerf.**

A kerf is a small cut made on the stone using a screwdriver or chisel to enable you to split the stone more accurately. For precision, create kerfs in the area you need to make the clean-cut, then use the rock hammer to break it through the kerfs.

- *To cut through fractures*

You will also use a rock hammer to cut through fractures in stones. A fracture is a weak stone point caused by several factors, like a drop or friction during smoothening.

Yes, you know the uses of a rock hammer, but are there precautions you should know?

Let's find out!

Precautions to Consider When Using a Rock Hammer

When using a rock hammer:

✓ Use a hammer that is of the right quality. Using low-quality hammers is ineffective and may also cause injury to your arm and wrist. Also, low-quality hammers may splinter during use, hence are a health hazard to you and the people around you.

✓ Use protective gear while working with the rock hammer. Protect your eyes using protective glasses to avoid injury from rock chips flying over as you work.

✓ Avoid using it as a chisel. That is, do not hit another hammer on the rock hammer to cut a stone. This prevents damaging the hammer and causing further fractures on the stone.

✓ Don't use it to cut brittle and precious stones. A rock hammer does not apply to all types of stones. For example, more precious stones like diamonds, emeralds, etc., require other tools to avoid too much damage and wastage. Also, using this tool on more brittle/delicate gemstones like opal would cause more harm than good.

- **Saws**

Another tool that you can use to cut rough stones is the saw.

There are two main types of saws, i.e., **slab saws** and **trim saws**.

i.   Slab Saw

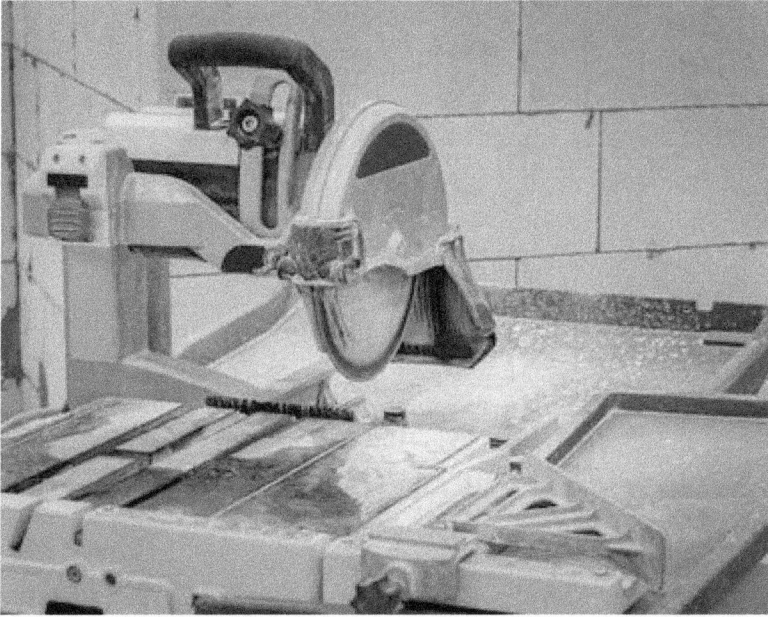

https://www.shutterstock.com/image-photo/stone-tile-cutting-machine-building-600nw-1701779431.jpg

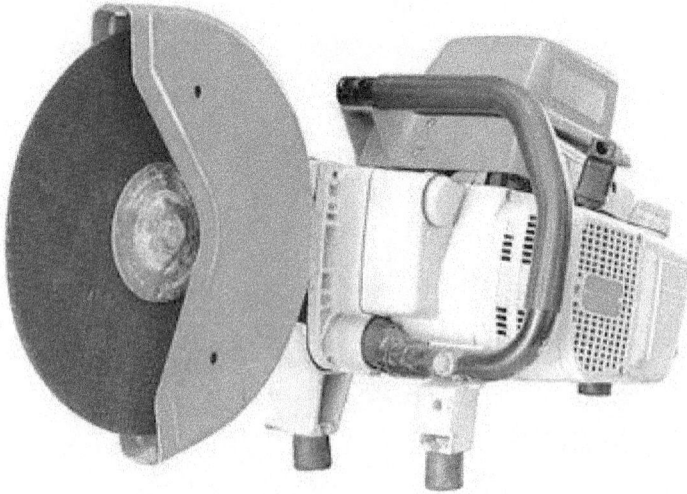

The slab saw has a diameter size of about 16-24 inches and is used to make straight cuts through larger stones, to form **slabs**. The good thing about its body is you can modify it in different ways that suit you.

The main features of the saw include:

✓ **The blade**- It cuts through the stones.

✓ **The saw tank**- Holds the lubricant, which lubricates the blades and other parts during the cutting process.

✓ **Coolant deflector**- It directs the flow of the coolant, which regulates the heat produced during the cutting process, hence keeping the temperatures in the cutting zone low.

✓ **Legs.** They support the saw, hence must be heavy enough to reduce vibration during cutting. However, some slab saws are placed on a solid surface like a table and do not come with supporting legs.

✓ **Arbor bearings**. It makes the rotation of the slab saw easy during cutting.

✓ **The hood**- It's made of steel and acts as a protective shield against loose chips during cutting. It also confines the coolant and lubricants so that there are no spills.

So, how do you use the slab saw?

How to Cut a Stone Using the Slab Saw

Here are the steps to follow:

- **Step 1: Feed the Saw**

To do this, place your stone in the correct position in front of the blade. The placement of the stone matters a lot because if you put it at the wrong angle, you may end up damaging the blade.

So, how do you feed the blade?

The blade and the stone should **run parallel** to each other.

Step 2: Lubricate the Saw

Once you feed the slab saw, the next step is to lubricate it.

Why?

Here is why:

✓ Lubricant oil to make the parts of the saw move with ease.

✓ The lubricant also prevents the blade from rusting.

Pour the grease onto the saw tank, which also holds water, but ensure it's the type designed for lapidary work.

When lubricating and using the slab saw, ensure you are in a well-ventilated room (or outdoors) to avoid intoxication. And, if lubricating the saw with the stone in place feels like too much work, you can do it as the first step.

Once it is all done, close the hood and run your saw. To ensure the stone is completely cut, let it run until the cut piece drops on the side of the blade (as shown in the image above).

- **Step 3: Clean the Saw**

After you have obtained the slab (cut stone) of your desired thickness, the next step would be to remove the residue on the blade and the tank to ensure the saw keeps functioning correctly.

From this point, the next step will be to use the trim saw to cut the slab into smaller pieces you will be working with.

ii.   Trim Saw

https://www.shutterstock.com/image-photo/milan-italy-may-11-2018-260nw-1872180511.jpg

Unlike the slab saw, the trim saw has thinner blades and is used to finely cut smaller pieces out of slabs and make desired shapes out of the stones. It does not have a hood, meaning you must have your safety gear (safety glasses, mask, apron, and gloves) on while working with it to protect yourself from loose chips. Also, you will have to use your hands to position the stones; hence it is essential to protect yourself from injury.

The main features of a trim saw are:

✓ **Diamond-tipped blade**- Used to cut the stones.

✓ **Clamp/vise**- It keeps the stone in place during cutting. Some trim saws, however, do not have the clamp. In such cases, you will have to use your hands to keep your stone in place. Keep your hands steady while performing this task if you get the trim saw without the clamp.

✓ **Tank**- For holding water and lubricant. When fixing the tank, remember to follow the manual so that it's easy to empty and clean after use.

So, how do you cut stones using a trim saw?

How To Use a Trim Saw

To cut using the trim saw:

• Start by **marking the stone** into the shapes you want to cut out. You may use a pencil to draw the shapes.

• **Pour the lubricant** into the tank and close it up.

- **Place your stone next to the blade**. If your trim saw has the clamp on, clamp your slab onto it, ensuring to position it well. If not, use your hands to hold the stone in place.

- Bring the blade to **cut through the marks** you made on your slab. What you produce from cutting the slab on the trim saw is known as **preforms** (shown in the image above).

The preforms made are now ready for the next processes, which we shall look at in the following chapters.

Chapter 3: Polishing Gem-stones-Tumbling

Do you ever wonder how precious stones are all shiny and smooth?

Well, one way of polishing gemstones is through a process referred to as **tumbling**, which uses the ancient concept of smoothing rocks along moving waters (like rivers). Tumbling, in simple terms, is defined as the stage in which precious/semiprecious rocks are smoothened into round and shiny stones.

During this process, you will use a rock tumbler, liquid lubricant, and abrasives as the primary equipment/tools.

So, what are they:

- **The Rock Tumbler**

This tool consists of the following:

✓ *A barrel.* This is the part where you put the preforms for tumbling. The barrel is lined with rubber to reduce vibration and prevent too much breakage of stones during tumbling.

✓ *Rotating rails* that support and turn the barrel around.

- ## The Lubricant

In most cases, water is used as the lubricant in the tumbling process. It's used to reduce friction on the rotating parts of the tumbler, hence reducing the heat generated during tumbling. It also makes it easier to move the abrasives in the barrel around more efficiently.

- ## The Abrasives

Also referred to as grit, the abrasive is a tool you can purchase or improvise by using tiny chips that break off from rough stones during the cutting process. Silicon carbide is the most commonly used type of grit in the lapidary world (Wikipedia[8]) due to its durability and availability.

However, even though the chips produced from rough stones during the cutting process play the same role, they may not be enough to do a thorough job.

During tumbling, the grit rubs against the preforms on all sides to produce a smooth and shapely gem.

So, let's look at the rock tumblers you will be working with.

Types of Rock Tumblers

There are two types of tumblers; the **rotary tumbler,** and the **vibratory tumbler**.

i.   The Rotary Rock Tumbler

https://www.shutterstock.com/image-photo/rock-tumbler-barrel-motion-260nw-1290709075.jpg

The rotary rock tumbler has a rotating barrel that turns around during tumbling. They are the most commonly used and are more readily available. Anyone with little skill in polishing stones can use them. Actually, with the right items, you can make one at home from scratch.

The rotary tumblers come in different sizes; you choose whichever suits you based on your work and budget. Some models have timers that you can set, while others operate manually.

The stones inside the barrel grind against each other as the barrel turns, creating a smooth finish. The longer the tumbler runs, the smoother the stones inside get. However, the time it takes to tumble also depends on the hardness of the stones.

ii.   The Vibratory Tumbler

https://www.shutterstock.com/image-photo/black-rubber-rock-tumbling-barrels-260nw-1514823674.jpg

This is another magnificent polishing tool. One of the unique characteristics of the vibratory tumbler is that it polishes stones and retains them in their existing shape, unlike the rotary tumbler, which gives your stones a rounded surface as they get polished.

Vibratory tumblers are used to polish more delicate/brittle stones. They are faster than rotary tumblers, taking almost one-third of the time the rotary tumbler takes. They also require fewer abrasives to polish.

When tumbling using the vibratory tumbler, use stones that have already been pre-shaped or on water-worn/riverbed pebbles to get the best results.

But does this rock tumbler have downsides?

Let's find out:

- ✓ The downside of the vibratory tumbler is that they are expensive to purchase and may not be ideal if your budget is tight.

- ✓ Again, unlike the rotary tumbler, whose barrel is lined with rubber, the vibratory tumbler has a plastic bowl, making the tumbling process quite noisy. It may, therefore, not be the best option to work with if you are doing lapidary from home or near other people's residences.

✓ While working with the vibratory tumbler, more supervision and inspection are needed. You will be required to open it up and check on any adjustments that need to be made frequently (at least two times a day). This is not the case with the rotary tumbler, as it can run continuously and effectively for up to four weeks.

Yes, you know the features and characteristics of the two main rock tumblers, but how do you choose the one that suits you?

Here is how:

Factors to Consider Before Buying a Rock Tumbler

Capacity

Image 1

Image 2

Twin vibratory (image 1) and rotary (image 2) rock tumblers (Source: Pinterest[9])

Tumblers are of different capacities. So, based on the work you want to accomplish, it is crucial to consider this.

For example, if you are polishing many stones, you don't want to choose a tumbler with a small capacity as this may require you to work on only a small batch at a time. In this case, a large-capacity tumbler is more effective as it takes an enormous load.

During tumbling, always load the barrel or bowl with the correct quantity, i.e., not more than three-quarters full. However, if you are tumbling fewer stones on a large tumbler, you must add tiny plastic beads or pellets to make the polishing more effective.

Some tumblers are designed in a way that they can run two barrels at a time. This increases the capacity, enabling you to double the output. Therefore, if you feel like a twin-barrel tumbler would go a long way to ease your work, then go for it.

Cost

What is your budget?

Are you prepared to spend a good chunk of money on a tumbler? Your answer to this question may be yes or no. Either way, you need to check on the different brands in the market and identify the one that best suits your needs. See if you can afford it.

As a beginner to the lapidary process, you may consider going for a more affordable one as you figure out how to care for it and give it the proper maintenance.

As we have seen before, vibratory tumblers are more expensive than rotary tumblers. If you are considering cost over speed, then the rotary rock tumbler may be better. It is, however, important to factor in the quality of the tumbler to cost. Some very cheap tumblers may not be long-lasting and require you to change or replace the parts often, which eventually becomes costly.

Type of Mineral/Stones to Work On

Generally, you can tumble nearly all types of gems in any rock tumbler. However, a few exceptions apply.

For example, some stones (like pearls) may be too brittle or delicate to be polished in a rotary tumbler. Others may require extra effort to bring out their rounded shape, which vibratory tumblers do not. However, this does not mean you cannot work on either type of tumbler. Instead, it means you get to choose the one that will be more functional based on the type of stones you will be dealing with.

Again, you need to consider the polishing material you will be using, depending on the stones you will be working with. It is preferable to use fine grit on vibratory tumblers and rougher grit on rotary tumblers.

Time Available for the Work

The time taken during tumbling depends on the hardness of the rocks, their roughness, and the extent of the smoothness/polish you desire, among other factors. Your availability to do the work will also affect your decision regarding the type of tumbler you intend to get.

If you don't have the patience to wait for weeks for a tumbling cycle to end, consider going for the vibratory tumbler. However, you will have to use stones that are not very rough. Also, you will need to be available during the process to monitor progress.

So, what are the steps/procedures followed during tumbling?

Here they are:

The Tumbling Process

✓ Load the barrel/bowl with your preforms.

✓ Add the abrasives and the lubricant/water.

✓ Place the barrel on the rotating rails of the rotary rock tumbler and allow it to rotate at the desired speed. The speed you use to tumble depends on the quantity of the contents in the barrel.

The tumbling concept uses the idea of smoothened stones on a river bed, i.e., a slow, long, but outstanding process. This means the tumbling process may take three to five weeks (or longer) to complete, based on the type of stones being tumbled and the abrasives used. However, if you are using the vibratory tumbler, it will take less time (one or two weeks).

Here are some powerful tips that will help make your tumbling process a success?

✓ To begin with, use coarse abrasives and load your tumbler to about half or not more than three-quarters of the total volume.

✓ Use stones of relatively similar hardness as the preforms.

✓ Once you start the tumbling process, you must listen for odd sounds indicating a malfunction. The tumbler should produce a steady sound all through. Keep the tumbling going for as long as is necessary.

✓ You may consider checking the progress after a few days and if you need to change the abrasives, do so. If necessary, add in finer abrasives for a better final polish.

✓ Every one or two weeks, clean up the barrel by filtering out the residue that has formed during the process. Clean up before changing to a finer abrasive. Cleaning up also involves sorting the stones. Separate those that require further tumbling from those that do not. You may use a colander for this purpose.

Sometimes, the tumbling process may require a final process that uses powdered polish. All you have to do is pour the polish into the barrel together with the water. Also, you will need to add some plastic pellets in the barrel to help carry the polish throughout the stones' surfaces and prevent too much wastage through chipping during the tumbling process.

Powdered Polish

Image 1   Image 2   Image 3

Cerium oxide (Image 1 source: polishing expert[10])

Tin oxide (Image 2 source: zoic Palaeotech[11])

Silicon carbide (source: eBay[12])

Powdered polish is usually made of tin oxide, silicon carbide, or cerium oxide and is available from different lapidary suppliers worldwide.

So, what are the uses of powdered polish?

Here they are:

- It polishes the stones, removing unwanted marks or blemishes from the preforms.

- It is used after the tumbling process for an additional smooth finish.

When using powdered polish, ensure the stones are smooth, i.e., they have already undergone the initial polishing process (tumbling).

Now, let's look at the different powdered polish:

✓ *Cerium oxide powder*

It is readily available and is used mainly for light or medium polishing due to its relative hardness. You can buy coarse or fine cerium oxide powder. The coarse one is ideal on relatively large stones and the fine on smaller pieces.

✓ *Tin oxide*

Tin oxide gives a gleaming finish to your stones. It can be used on its own or as a mixture of other powder polishes. This powder works best on rocks like quartz, marble, or granite, and the amount you use depends on how long the rocks will take in the tumbler and the extent of the smoothness you need.

✓ *Silicon carbide*

Silicon carbide is rugged and durable, and despite being a polishing powder, it is popularly used as an abrasive. It is synthetic, making it readily available, and hence commonly used by lapidarists to polish stones.

Other powdered polishes available in the market and can also be used effectively include synthetic diamond, diamond powder, aluminum oxide, and powdered gemstones.

As stated earlier, how you tumble your stones depends on their hardness, so let's look at how to measure the hardness or softness of rocks.

Determining the Hardness of Stones

Mohs Hardness Scale

Mineral Name	Scale Number	Common Object
Diamond	10	
Corundum	9	Masonry Drill Bit (8.5)
Topaz	8	
Quartz	7	Steel Nail (6.5)
Orthoclase	6	
Apatite	5	Knife/Glass Plate (5.5)
Fluorite	4	Copper Penny (3.5)
Calcite	3	
Gypsum	2	Fingernail (2.5)
Talc	1	

Increasing Hardness

Source: National Park Service[13]

To compare the hardness of stones/minerals, you have to scratch them against other substances whose hardness is known. The scale used to measure hardness is known as the **Mohs Hardness Scale**. It ranges from a scale of 1-10, with 1 being the least and 10 being the hardest.

Silicon carbide, for instance, has a Mohs hardness of 9, and diamond (the hardest natural mineral) is a Mohs of 10.

As a beginner in the lapidary journey, you may use readily available objects like steel nails or knives to determine the hardness of your stones with the guide of the Mohs Hardness Scale.

What does this mean?

A stone can only scratch those that are below it on the scale.

Tumble rocks of similar or relatively similar hardness together. For the abrasives, find those of greater hardness than the stones you are tumbling.

From there, let's get to the next lapidary stage.

Chapter 4: Cabbing

Image 1

Image 1: Cabochons (Source: kernowcraft.com[14])

Image 2   Image 3

Image 2: Image of agate stone showing a variety of colors in it (Source: ahsapkolsaati.com[15])

Image 3: Sapphires cut out into cabochons (Source: diamondbuzz.blog[16])

To you, a beginner, the word cabbing may be unfamiliar. The process is, however, one of the most common in the art of gem-cutting and is an easy-to-do, fun activity that does not require training.

So, what is cabbing?

This activity in the lapidary world involves shaping gemstones into rounded forms. With cabbing, the top part of the stone becomes domed/convex while the bottom stays flat. Once the rocks have been cut, polished, and shaped into rounded tops, you refer to them as **cabochons** (as shown in image 1 above).

Cabochons are mainly crafted from opaque and relatively soft stones as they are easier to shape and polish. Some stones used to make cabochon through the cabbing process include agate, quartz, and other semiprecious stones of Mohs hardness 7 or below. Stones with various colors usually make more impressive and interesting cabochon pieces than those with only one color.

Other stones with unique features, like sapphires (though a hard rock of Mohs hardness 9), are also used in cabochon-making. The process makes the features in the stones stand out better (as shown in image 3 above).

So, how is the cabbing process done?

The Step-By-Step Process of Cabbing

Here are the steps to follow when cabbing your stones:

Step 1: Choose the Right Stones to Work With

Asterism effect   Chatoyance effect

Source: Jewellermagazine.com[17]

The first step in cabochon involves choosing the suitable stone for the job. As we have seen previously, some stones work better with cabochons than others. You can buy large slabs and use the slab and trim saws to cut them into preforms, or you may purchase the already cut stones.

Some of the other factors to consider when buying stones for cabbing are:

✓ Hardness.

✓ Opaqueness. Opaque or translucent stones produce better cabochons than transparent ones because they reveal the beauty hidden in the rocks.

✓ Fractures or pits. A good piece should be free from cracks, holes, or fractures to avoid too much wastage.

✓ Design/patterns/Color/Composition: For best results, use stones with different patterns, colors, and compositions. Some patterns or colors on the rocks may create an **asterism** or a **chatoyancy** effect on your cabochon, increasing its worth. An asterism effect is when the gem brings out a star-shaped formation (that turns round) from the reflection of light. A chatoyancy effect (also known as the **cat's eye**) is when the cabochon displays one band of light on its surface and turns as light reflects at different angles.

Step 2: Stencil, Ready for Cutting

Image 1

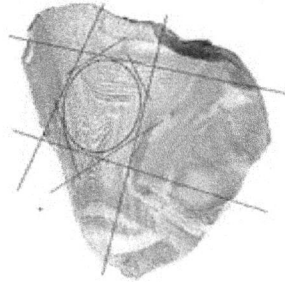

Image 2

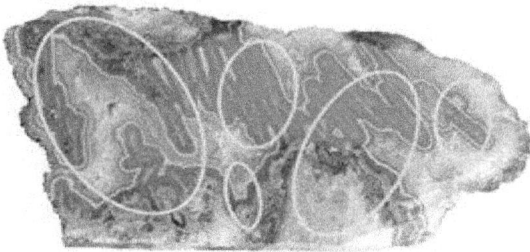

Image 3

Image 1:An example of a stencil template (Source: printables.com[18])

Image 2: An example of a marked slab (Source: gemsociety.org[19])

Image 3: Source: cabking.com[20]

When you have the slabs, you must study the features carefully to get the best preforms. Stones have top and bottom sides, and as you decide the shapes you want your cabochons to take, consider the unique patterns and colors on both sides of the stone. Take advantage of each of the patterns, colors, and designs so that you make maximum use of your slab. This means that you've got to be thoughtful and creative.

Study the stones first to have a picture of the end product in your mind. Then, draw shapes using a stencil template and a pencil (or aluminum pen if available), considering both the top and bottom of your cabochon.

Some templates come in doubles to make marking both sides of the slab easier. Others also come in sets, giving you several ideas to choose from.

It is important to note that you can make stencils from what is available. For example, you may cut out shapes from cardboard and use them in case other stencil templates are unavailable.

Image 2 above shows a slab that has been marked. The oval shape is made using a template, while the straight markings show where you will cut, being deliberate to reduce wastage as much as possible.

Image 3 shows a colorful slab (top side) stenciled to bring out the best from its patterns.

Step 3: Cut the Shapes Out

Once you have outlined your slab with your stencil, the next step is to cut the shapes out.

What do you use?

A trim saw cuts close to the stencil lines. However, it can only make straight lines. When cutting out, do so close to the stencil markings but not directly on them. Leave some extra material, which you will trim in the following processes.

Focus on minimizing wastage as much as you can. Remember, the pieces you cut out can also be used to cut other preforms that you can shape, polish, and make other beautiful pieces.

You will reveal more features on the stones as you cut the shapes. It is easier to cut opaque rocks (for example, an opaque emerald) since they only have one color and can be cut at any angle. When cutting, be careful not to trim out patterns or colors that would make your cabochon more valuable.

Once you have cut the shapes out, clean up the preforms using warm water and soap to remove the grim and dirt that may have accumulated. The preforms are now ready for shaping (cabbing).

Step 4: Cabochon Shaping

The process of shaping the cabochon uses a machine called a **grinder**. In this step, you may use a **dop stick** (a process referred to as **doping**) or shape using only the grinder and your hands to turn the stone around on the wheel.

Remember, where the stone/slab is large, you will have to cut it using a trim saw to help save time on the grinder. This also prevents too much wastage as you can use the cut stones to make other smaller cabochons or gems.

So, let's look at the steps, tools, and terms used in this shaping process:

Doping

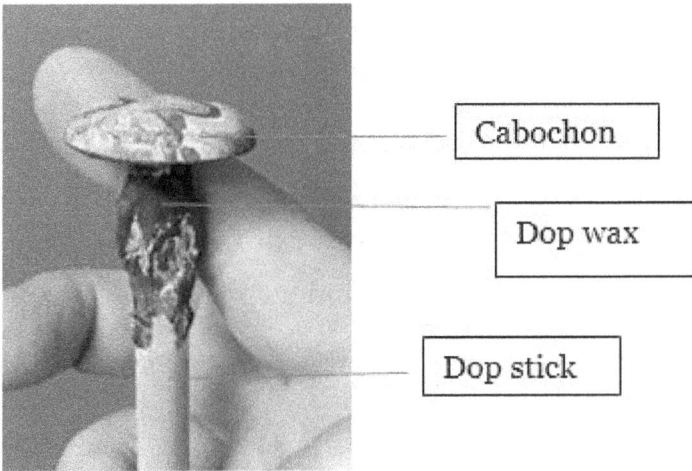

Cabochon

Dop wax

Dop stick

A cabochon stone stuck on a dop stick (Source: gotcharocks.com[21])

What is doping?

This is where cut stones, ready for cabbing, are adhered on a long wooden or metallic stick using tough wax, then run on the grinder. The stick is known as a **dop stick,** while the wax is referred to as the **cabbing/dop wax.**

The dop stick protects your fingers from the grinding machine. It also makes handling the preforms easier and creates more precise shapes from the stones. However, it is not a compulsory technique; you can still use your hands and bring out a perfectly-shaped cabochon.

The dop wax is hard at room temperature but moldable and soft above room temperature.

So, how do you fix a cabochon on the dop stick?

Here is how:

✓ To fix a cabochon on the dop stick, heat the wax to about 50 degrees Celsius on a dop pot, and heat the cabochon to the same temperature.

✓ Then, dip the stick inside the molded wax and fix it on the stone.

✓ Press the wax onto the stone with your fingers. Make sure to fix the dop stick on the bottom side of the stone. It is, however, essential to note that dop sticks might not be effective if you are cabbing relatively large pieces of rocks.

Where dop wax is not available, you can go for **Gorilla super glue** as it plays the same role as the wax. It is also easier to use since you will not need to heat it or the stone as you press the stone on the stick. The only downside of the glue is that it is not as easy to take out the dop-stick once done compared to the dop wax.

Once you have fixed the stick on the stone, you can begin grinding.

Grinding

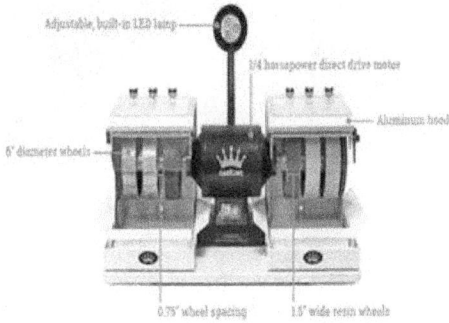

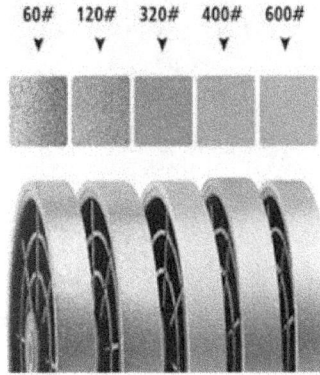

Image 1

Image 2

Image 1: An example of a grinder (Source: gravescompany.com[22])

Image 2: Wheels (Source: aliexpress.com[23])

 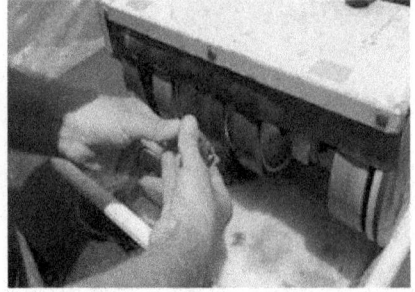

Image 3   Image 4

Image 3: Cabbing process using a dop stick (source: cabking.com24)

Image 4: Cabbing using hands to hold (source: youtube25)

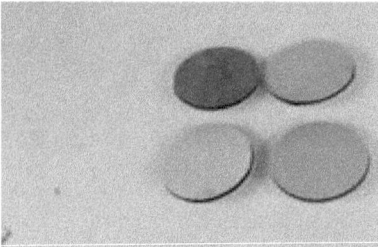

Image 5

Image 5: Polishing pads (source: diamondpacific.com26)

Polishing pad on a cabbing machine

Image 6

Image 6: Source: youtube.com[27]

The main equipment used to make cabochons is the grinder, also called the **grinding wheel, grinding machine,** or **cabbing machine**. There are, however, various other tools and items that you will be required to have to make your cabbing work successful.

For example, you will need a dop pot to help with doping. Also, you must put on your safety gear (gloves, eyeglasses, etc.) while cabbing.

Here, we will discuss what you need to know about the grinding machine.

The machine brings out the uniqueness and beauty of cabochons by grinding, sanding, shaping, and polishing them.

How does it do this?

It uses discs (also called wheels) that contain grit of varying fineness. A grinding machine can have between two to six discs, and each disc plays a different role, depending on its class. The harder stones use the coarse disc, whereas the softer stones use the finer disc.

Image 1 above shows a more advanced type of cabbing machine. The motor helps run the machine, and the hood protects you against splashes from water and residue. On the other hand, the LED lamp provides close-up lighting while working, whereas the water pump and removable trays on either side are where the residue settles. The trays make cleaning more manageable. The diameter and resin wheels are of varying coarseness.

The numbers shown in image 2 above represent the **grit size** on the wheels, which is determined by the abrasive edges glued on the wheels' surfaces. Bigger grit sizes have more abrasive edges on the wheels, and the smaller the sizes of the particles on the abrasive, the finer the wheel. The abrasives used on the wheels could be *silicon carbide, diamond grit*, or any other material. The shapes also differ in some machines, with some wheels convex shapes and others concave.

60-grit size (60#) is for rough stones. As you go on grinding, move on to the next grit-size wheel until you get the smoothness required. Some cabbing machines have wheels that go up to grit size 3000 (3000#, a very fine wheel with tiny abrasive particles).

The wheels rotate at high speed, allowing you to shape the gemstones as you move along. Moving from one wheel to the other removes the scratches formed from the previous grit-size wheel. You may use a dop stick on your gem during the process, especially for the small stones, or you could shape using your hands. However, be careful when using your hands, so you do not end up sanding off your fingertips.

Also, remember that when the wheels rotate, water will drip onto them to lubricate the surface and prevent dust from flying off. Therefore, you should not cab without feeding water on the wheels.

When you complete a step on each wheel, clean the stone and wipe it dry.

Why?

Here is why:

✓ It helps you see the scratches, giving you an idea of where to start on the next wheel.

✓ It also ensures you do not transfer dust particles on the next wheel.

However, remember to take note of the template markings you made on your stone and grind along them as you move on to the finer wheels.

So, what do you do once you shape your stones?

• Once you obtain the shape you want, **pre-polishing** will be the next step. This involves applying the wheels with a fine grit to prepare the stones for the final polishing stage. When doing this, ensure your stone is clean and dry, and polish it until no more scratches are visible.

• Then, you will be ready to move on to the **polishing stage**. Apply polishing agents such as tin oxides, diamond paste, chromium oxide, or cerium oxide (usually in paste) on polishing pads such as **canvas, leather pads, or felt** (shown in images 5 and 6 above). During this step, polish the stones until you get the desired smoothness. It is important to note that the polishing process will not remove any materials on your cabochon.

So, if there are scratches, you need to return to the cabbing wheels to get rid of them.

- Once done with the process, clean up your machine.

Flat lap

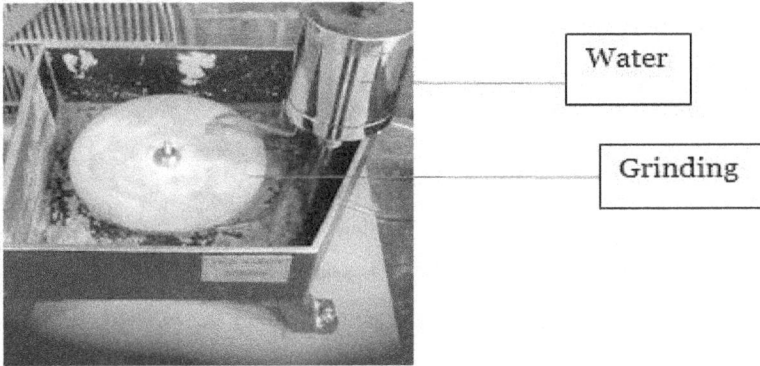

Water

Grinding

Image 1

Image 1: Image of a flat lap (source: smls.online[28])

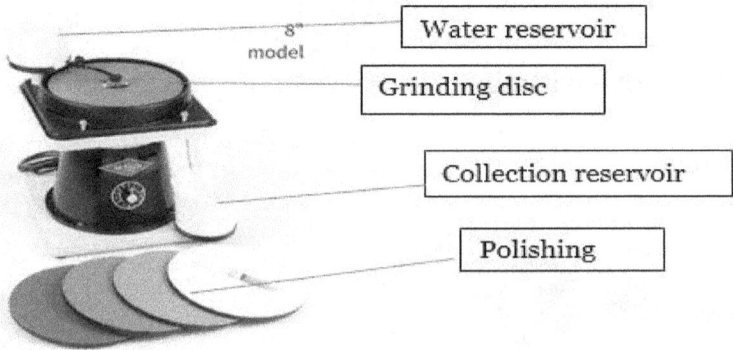

8"
model

Water reservoir

Grinding disc

Collection reservoir

Polishing

Image 2

Image 2: Image of a more advanced flat lap (Source: hitechdiamond.com[29])

Image 3

Image 3: Simple homemade flat lap (Source: Rock Tumbling Hobby[30])

Another lapidary tool used in cabbing is the **flat lapidary grinding machine**, also referred to as the **flat lap** or **rotary flat lap**. It plays the same role as the grinding machine but is relatively less complex, becoming ideal for beginners. The flat lap is more affordable than the grinding machine and easy to install and work with.

You can purchase a flat lap from the stores; the cost depends on its distinct features. You may also choose to build one yourself from the available materials around you. Image 3 above shows a simple homemade flat lap. Find more ideas on this at 186 More Best Homemade Tools[31].

So, what are some of the uses of the flat lap?

✓ It grinds, smoothens, and polishes stones to form cabochons.

✓ It also works well in creating a flat bottom or base on a cabochon onto which you will stick it to the mount.

Flat lap uses **discs**, also called **laps**, whose grit is of varying coarseness. The grit can be of silicon carbide or diamond. A diamond grit is more effective and lasts longer, but if you cannot find one, the silicon carbide grit will still do the job.

Like the rotary cabbing machine, you must feed this machine with water, in the water reservoir, during use. The water drips onto the grinding disc slowly to lubricate the surface, then collects in another bucket (the collection reservoir) for discarding. You find that, unlike with the cabbing machine, the water on the flat lap does not create a lot of mess since only small drips are released while working.

So, how do you use the flat lap?

Here is how:

- To shape the cabochon, use a circular rotation with the dop stick and keep checking to see if you have achieved the desired dome shape. Begin from the more coarse disc, and move on to the finer ones as your cabochon forms its shape. Remember to clean up your cabochon before moving on to the next disc to ensure that you don't transfer coarse grit to the finer discs (**"cross-contamination"**).

- As you continue to shape, identify flat areas on the cabochon and work on them. Go as far as you can, but do not overdo it so that you do not damage the stone or cause too much damage.

- Once satisfied with your results, it is time to **polish** the cabochons. Polishing agents used in this process are mainly tin oxide, diamond paste, or cerium oxide. You may need to test the agents on your stones to see which one suits it, depending on the type of stone you are working with. Remember to keep the water dripping on the flat lap as you polish until you get the desired results.

- Clean up the machine once you have completed the process.

From here, let's get to the next lapidary stage.

Chapter 5: The Carving Process

Image 1

Image 2

Image 1: Carving made out of agate stone (Source: proantic.com[32])

Image 2: Jade stone carving (Source: USC US-China Institute website[33])

Have you ever come across gemstones that have engraved images on them? Or some that are shaped into attractive designs through chiseling? If the answer to these questions is yes, you may know what carving in lapidary is about.

It is a lapidary art process requiring much more creativity than processes like tumbling or cabochon-making. However, it is not as complex as it may appear, and you may be surprised how creative you can be at carving stones!

So, what exactly is carving?

It involves creating shapes on a stone by scraping, chipping off, or cutting away materials from it. Sometimes, it is referred to as **hardstone carving** to differentiate carving involving the use of gemstones/semiprecious stones from the one that involves other materials like soap-stones, marble, and limestones, among others. Other sources[34] refer to gemstone carving also as **glyptic art**.

Using a creative mind and the right tools, you may carve out simple designs or make them as complicated as you desire. Lapidarists specializing in this art consider this process a "free form," requiring more of your imagination than precision or angles.

Now, let's dig deeper into the process, to have a better understanding of this art.

Tools used in the Carving Process

First, like with the other lapidary processes, you must have safety gear while carving your stones.

Do you remember them?

Wear your dust mask to avoid inhaling harmful dust particles, safety glasses to protect your eyes from flying stone pieces, and protective gloves for your fingers' safety.

Besides the safety gear, you need tools to help you work efficiently.

These are:

1. Hand Saws

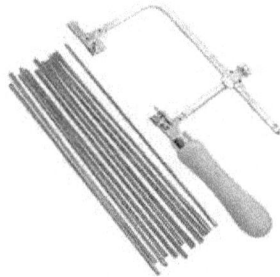

Image 1   Image 2

Image 3

Image 1: Piercing frame saw (source: eternaltools.com35)

Image 2: Frame saw with different types of blades (source: pinterest.com36)

Image 3: Image illustrating how the diamond wire saw blade is used (source: eternaltools.com37)

They are two commonly used hand saws: **piercing frame** and **diamond wire saws**. These saws are used to cut parts of a stone and carve out shapes through the back-and-forth motion.

As a lapidarist, you will be required, in addition, to use a marker or **grease pencil/Chinagraph pencil** while working with the hand saws. The pencil or marker makes the appropriate markings on your stone to guide you where to carve out without staining it.

The hand saws are adjustable to fit the different-sized blades/wires.

2. Diamond Drill Bits

Image 1

Image 2

Image 3

Image 1: Diamond drill bits of different sizes

Image 2: Diamond core drill bits

Image 3: Twisted diamond drill bits

Images source: eternaltools.com[38]

Stone carving involves drilling holes to produce designs, and one of the best tools to use is the diamond drill bit. You've got to use a drilling/cutting material higher on the Mohs hardness scale than the stone you are cutting/drilling. Since the diamond is the highest on the scale, the diamond tip on the bit makes it perfect for drilling even hard stones.

The drill bits come in different sizes and shapes, each bringing out varying and unique designs. They are also coated differently; some have only one diamond coating, and you must replace the bit once it wears off. Others have **electroplated diamond drill bits**, while the more advanced ones (**the sintered diamond drill bits**) have more than one diamond coating and last longer.

Use diamond drills with significant bits for large incisions, while for small incisions and more detailed designs, go for the small diamond drill bits. During this process, you don't need to drill underwater, even though some lapidarists do so to reduce the dust blowing off.

The diamond drill bits in image 2 above are known as the **diamond core drill bits**. They are hollow, making it easier to create designs as water runs through to lubricate, cool the drill and help clean up the residue. They also come in different sizes.

Another type is the **twisted diamond drill bits** (shown in image 3 above). They are mainly used to increase the size of existing holes in a gem/semiprecious stone.

3. Diamond burrs

Image 1   Image 2

Image 1: V-wheel-shaped diamond burr (Image source: Cutting Edge Supply co[39])

Image 2: Cylinder-head diamond burr (source: Cutting Edge Supply Co[40])

Another set of tools that come in handy to make beautiful engravings on a gemstone is the diamond burrs. As a lapidarist, you will use it to cut and shape stones, creating forms or designs that your imaginative and artistic mind allows.

So, how do you use the diamond burrs?

You will have to fix the diamond drill bits and the burrs onto a **Dremel rotary tool**. The Dremel rotary tool (referred to as Dremel) is plugged into a power supply and rotates your drill bits and burrs as you work.

4. Dremel Rotary Tool

Image of a Dremel rotary tool with the different diamond tips used on it (source: rockseeker.com[41])

The best Dremels have motors whose speed can be adjusted.

To make carvings on a stone using the Dremel, you must begin with a slow speed, then move to higher speeds depending on the precision you want to achieve and the type of stone you are carving.

Are there tips you need to know when using the Dremel?

Let's find out:

✓ First, clean your stones before you begin carving and ensure no residue is on their surface.

✓ Again, keep them wet when working with the Dremel so that dust particles do not blow off. However, be cautious when using water to prevent shock if using a Dremel that is electric-powered or corded.

When using the Dremel, these are additional accessories you must have to help make the carving process successful.

Are you wondering which ones?

Here they are:

- *Polishing and buffing wheels*

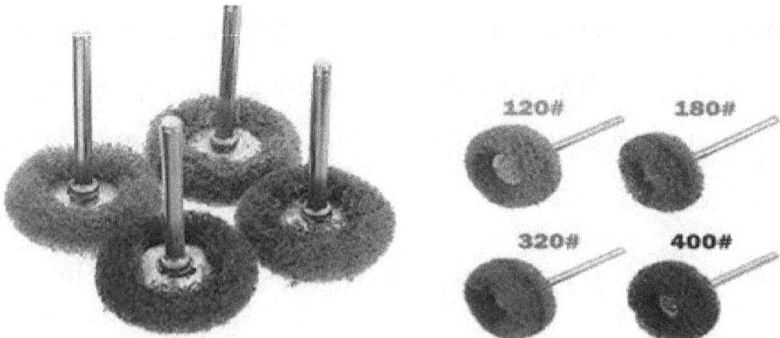

Polishing and buffing wheels (source: amazon.com[42])

As the name suggests, you will use these wheels to polish your pieces, giving them a shiny and attractive finish. The wheels come in various grit sizes ranging from 120# to 400# (as shown in image 2 above), and as usual, you begin from the coarsest and move on to the finest to make your polishing thorough.

The wheels are available in different diameters. Usually, they come in a set containing different diameters and grit sizes. Wheels with small diameter heads will help you buff inside grooves easily.

- *Diamond polishing paste*

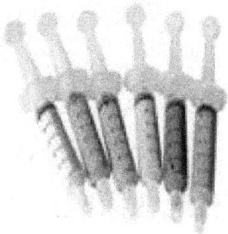

Diamond polishing paste in syringes for easier application. (Source: eternaltools.com43)

To produce the perfect finish, use the polishing wheels with **diamond paste** or any other **polishing agent** in the final polishing step. The paste is usually mixed with water to obtain the right consistency and then applied to the stone using a syringe. Once applied, the wheel brushes through the rock to produce a scratch-free mirror finish.

- *Hand polishing pad*

Diamond resin hand-polishing pads of different grit sizes (source: amazon.com44)

We all know that gemstone artwork is not complete without polishing. If polishing wheels are unavailable, you can still polish your piece with the hand polishing pads.

These unique pads are made of resin and coated with diamond grit. They are relatively more affordable than the diamond polishing wheels and come in handy during the stone-carving process. Like the wheels, the pads also come in varying grit sizes.

They are ideal for smoothening off curved edges due to their flexibility. However, remember always to use them on wet surfaces.

With your tools, safety gear, and stones ready, let's learn how to go about the carving process.

The Carving Technique

In this stage, we will look at how to make actual carvings the two main ways, namely: **Cameo** and **Intaglio**.

Let's see what each of them involves:

Cameo

Cameo image on agate stone (source: the-maac.com45)

Cameo is the process of engraving objects or pictures on a gemstone (or other materials) to display a raised effect on the image. The raised effect is referred to as **positive relief** in the carving process.

A positive relief image will, in most cases, but not always, have a different background color than the image itself. This aspect came about because lapidarists and carvers would carve out materials in the background and leave out where they would engrave the image. Since many hardstones have layers of different colors, exposing the inner layers by carving out the outer ones brings out a positive relief effect.

For example, in the image above, two contrasting colors meet, i.e., white meets a dark background color.

Sometimes, you may leave the colors as they naturally appear on your piece; other times, you may enhance the contrast by dyeing.

So, how do you carve your stone using the cameo techniques?

Using your hands, sketch out the image, curve out the details of the image with drill bits and burrs, then polish it.

Intaglio

Agate stone on the gold ring with an intaglio image engraved (source: pinterest.com46)

Also known as an **engraved gem**, intaglio (the letter "g" is silent in pronunciation), in simple terms, is the opposite of cameo. It is an engraved gem, in which the design is etched/inscribed into the surface of the top side of the stone. Intaglio produces a **negative relief image**.

So, how does this technique work?

✓ You will use the different diamond drill bits and burrs to perform the incision job once you have made your markings. Ensure you use the right bits to bring out your image's details to get the desired result.

✓ Once done, use your polishing wheels or pads for that final mirror finish.

So, what other processes do your gemstones have to go through?

Let's find out!

Chapter 6: Faceting

Image 1

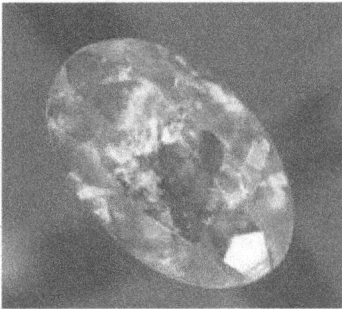

Image 2

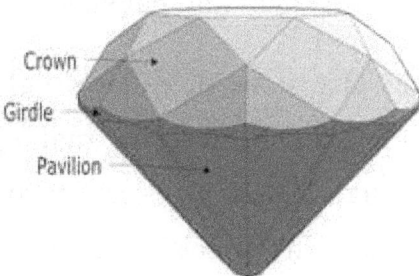

Image 3

Image 1: A faceted gem and a cabochon (source: edwardflemingjewellery.com[47])

Image 2: Faceted opal (source: pinterest.com[48]).

Image 3: a sample of the general overview of a faceted stone (Image source: langantiques.com[49]).

Another exciting and fun process in producing great pieces from gemstones is the process of **faceting**. And even though it may sound like a complicated technique for you as a beginner, it is worth your effort. Some designs may require more advanced skills, while others are relatively easy to work on.

Now, what exactly is faceting?

It involves cutting gemstones at specific angles to make different flat surfaces called **facets**. The difference between cabbing and faceting is that a cabochon has a rounded finish, while faceted stone has many straight edges and flat sides.

Since a faceted stone has many flat sides, it reflects light better, giving it a beautiful sparkling finish. However, making facets is not as simple as making cabochons because you must work on the angles and sides with precision. For this reason, faceted stones are more expensive than cabochons.

Like in other processes, when faceting, you need to take great care to not lose a lot of material as you cut.

Additional factors to consider before faceting a gemstone include:

- *The features*

Some gemstones are better as cabochons than facets. For example, if a rough stone has too many natural imperfections like bubbles or breakage lines (fissures), then make a cabochon. If faceted, the piece will not reflect light as desired and, therefore, will be unattractive.

- *The color*

Transparent or translucent stones reflect light better and are best faceted, while dark-colored gemstones are ideal for making cabochons. Quartz and diamond produce great pieces when faceted as they are translucent. Other stones with lighter shades/tones of color are opal, topaz, emerald, and tourmaline.

- *The cut*

You also need to study your stone to be able to understand at what angle you are going to cut the facets. If you use the wrong angle sizes on a rock, the result may not be suitable. We shall touch on this as we learn how to facet your stones.

But how does a faceted stone look?

Image 3 above shows a general overview of how a stone is faceted.

The crown is the top part of the stone, **the girdle** is the middle part which separates the top from the bottom, and **the pavilion** is the lower part. When fixing a faceted gemstone on an ornament, the crown mostly becomes the visible part, while the pavilion is where the stone will rest on the ornament.

So, what equipment should you have when faceting?

Faceting Equipment

You may wonder what equipment you need as a beginner to succeed in the faceting art. Well, we will look at the tools of this process here to enable you confidently venture into this fantastic opportunity.

Before going out of your way to buy the equipment, consider the following factors:

✓ Buy what is essential, i.e., what you cannot do without. As a beginner, you don't have to buy all the equipment you saw at an expert's place. Save yourself some money by purchasing the most important ones first; then, as you gain more experience, you will add more to your workshop. This book will help you identify the equipment you must have when starting.

✓ Consider the type and brand to source from. If possible, seek the guidance of a lapidarist near you because hands-on practice will help you know the best equipment in terms of functionality and quality.

✓ If going for used (second-hand) equipment, ensure all parts are working and if some need replacing, find out first if they are available in the market before you commit yourself to buy the equipment. Before buying used equipment, compare refurbishing costs to purchasing new ones.

Here are the primary tools and equipment used in faceting:

Main Faceting Tools and Equipment

1. Faceting Machine

Image 2

Image 1

Image 1 and image 2: images of two different faceting machines (source: gemsociety.org⁵⁰)

Image 3

Image 3: Different parts of a faceting machine (source: gemsociety.org[51])

The faceting machine is one of the pieces of equipment you must have to facet your stones. You can buy a simple or more sophisticated type, depending on the type of stones you are working on. As a beginner, you do not have to start with expensive stones like diamonds that require a particular faceting machine. Instead, you can work with stones like quartz, beryl, topaz, or opal.

So, what are some of the essential features of a faceting machine?

✓ Most faceting machines have a fitted yet adjustable **protractor** that helps cut your stones at the correct angle.

✓ It has **an indicator dial** that helps you to make error-free cuts.

✓ The machine has **a drip water system** to lubricate and cool the work surface.

✓ It also has **a drainage system** which drains out dirty water into an outlet.

2. Dop Sticks and Dop Wax

You will need dop sticks and dop wax for faceting.

Why?

The dop wax will help stick your stones on the dop sticks before attaching them to your machine. Some faceting machines come with a set of dop sticks of varying shapes and sizes, which make your work easier.

You will need a source of heat like a spirit burner or candle to heat the stones and the wax to make it easy to fix the stone onto the dop stick.

3. Diamond and Copper Laps

These are attached to the faceting machine to help cut and polish your stones. Most machines come with these laps, but you can still buy additional ones depending on the grit size you intend to have.

In addition to the diamond and copper laps, you need to have **metal-bonded laps**. These laps are excellent at producing clean facets and are made of copper discs and coated with diamond powder. The diamond powder is used to polish the gemstones once the cutting process is complete.

You will need synthetic diamond powder of grit size 1200-3000 at the pre-polishing stage and around 100000 at the polishing stage.

4. Calipers

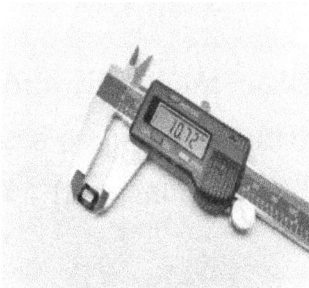

Digital caliper (source: dreamstime.com[52])

You will need calipers to make accurate measurements of your faceted stone. Calipers measure rock sizes, thus helping you know how much you have after the cutting and polishing steps. The most used type is the **digital caliper**.

Even though this equipment is not a must-have, it is still very functional.

With your tools and equipment ready, let's get to the faceting process.

How Facet Your Stones

Once you have identified what tools and equipment you need to facet your stone, the next step will be learning the actual faceting procedure to obtain the perfect pieces.

So, here are the steps to follow:

Step 1: Choose Your Stone

Choose the rough stone you want to work on, then study it to identify where you want the crown and the pavilion to sit. Ensure you observe the different tones, inclusions, and all other vital features on your rough stone.

Step 2: Clean and pre-shape the stone

Use a grinding lap and your hands to clean and slightly pre-shape your stone.

Step 3: Fix The Dop Stick to The Faceting Machine

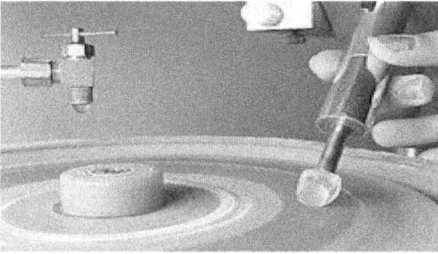

Source: Wikipedia53

During this step:

✓ First, change the lap to a faceting diamond lap.

✓ Attach the rough stone to the dop stick using the dop wax. Remember to heat the wax and the surface of the rock on which you will be sticking the dop stick to ensure the wax properly adheres.

✓ Fix the dop stick onto the quill on the faceting machine. Adjust its height so that the stone touches the lap; not too low to cause wastage and not too high to make poor cuts (as shown in the image above).

Step 4: Set The Machine on The Appropriate Angle and Index

Round Brilliant Cut

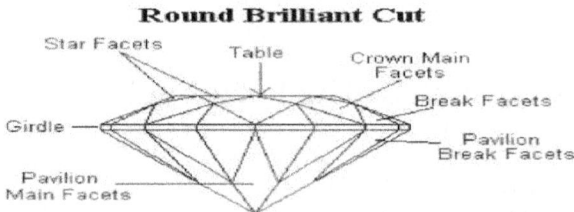

Facets	Angle	Pavilion Settings Index
Pavilion Mains	42°	96 12 24 36 48 60 72 84
Girdle	90°	94 86 82 74 70 62 58 50 46
		38 34 26 22 14 10 2
Break Facets	43.7°	94 86 82 74 70 62 58 50 46
		38 34 26 22 14 10 2
		Crown Settings
Crown Mains	35°	0 12 24 36 48 60 72 84
Break Facets	37.5°	2 10 14 22 26 34 38 46 50
		58 62 70 74 82 86 94
Star Facets	16°	6 18 30 42 54 66 78 90
Table	0°	

Source: gemsociety.org54

This depends on the type of stone you are working with. Set the machine on the appropriate angle and index for the first facet. Use the table above to help you do so. During this step, try to be as precise as possible, as the cut angles will determine the amount of light reflected on the stone and the sparkle produced thereof.

To cut a round facet, for example, you will have eight pavilion mains, each at an angle of 42 degrees, 16 girdles at 90 degrees, and 16 break facets at 43.7 degrees. For the first pavilion facet, cut at index 96, then proceed as shown in the diagram above.

Step 5: Start The Faceting Process

When you get to this step:

✓ Turn on the water and start faceting.

✓ Begin on the pavilion, then to the girdle, the break facets, and finally to the crown main and star facets. The final side to work on is the table. Let the stone on the dop stick move back and forth as the machine makes the cuts but do not use too much pressure. Also, the speed should not be too high.

✓ Cut until you notice the change in the sound produced. This is an effective way to know when you have made a proper cut. When the stone is cut to the set angle and index, the grinding noise should reduce to a clicking sound.

✓ When one side is complete, turn the stone and work on the next side. Cut all the sides, adjusting your index and angles appropriately. Every once in a while, pause to inspect your facets. Make proper adjustments where need be.

Step 6: Pre-Polish your Stone

Once you are satisfied with your facets, it is time to pre-polish the stone.

How?

✓ First, clean up the stone and the machine.

✓ Replace the grinding laps with the polishing laps.

✓ Polish all through, pausing every once in a while to check the progress.

Step 7: Polish the Facet

Source: gemologyproject.com55

The final faceting step is polishing the gems. Apply diamond paste (or any other polishing agent) on a grit-less lap, then use it to polish the facet. The final product should be a bright, sparkling, and beautiful gem, as shown in the image above.

As stated earlier, faceting is a bit hard; hence, as a beginner, you may not get the desired results initially. However, just like with all other hobbies, practice makes perfect. The idea is to keep going, keep practicing, and have the desire to learn from your mistakes. Soon, you will be able to produce extraordinary pieces worth your time and effort.

Let's now dig in more and learn a few more tips that will come in handy during your lapidary journey.

Chapter 7: How to Correctly Identify a Gem or Semiprecious stone

As we come to the end of the study on lapidary processes, we need to highlight the main characteristics of gemstones and semiprecious stones. This is information you must have at your fingertips to become an expert.

So,

How do you distinguish a precious stone from other materials with similar physical features?

A gemstone is a natural mineral used to make high-quality and valuable jewelry. Yes, these stones are mined, and in most cases, they have naturally occurring imperfections, but they are still considered gemstones. Gemstones are treated to enhance their beauty while retaining their mineral composition.

But do you need to consider before identifying a stone as precious/semiprecious?

Characteristics of Precious/Semiprecious Stones

Here are the characteristics of gems/semiprecious stones:

Rarity

Precious stones are rare in nature. Most expensive gemstones like diamonds, sapphire, ruby, and emeralds are not readily available.

The Color

Gemstones have an attractive color. At first, you might find it hard to differentiate between a real and a fake gem. If/when this happens, it would be essential to consult a trustworthy lapidarist with more experience in the field. An experienced lapidarist is likely to distinguish an imitation from a real gem.

Inclusions

Most valuable gemstones are free from artificially occurring inclusions. Natural gemstones may contain inclusions like insects, and cracks, among others, in them. On the other hand, synthetic materials like glass may have air bubbles, making it easy to tell their worth.

Light Reflection

For most natural gemstones, light reflects the same color as the stone. But for the synthetic ones, the light is reflected in different colors.

You know how to identify gems, but does this mean they are the only stones you have to use?

Well, let's find out!

Can A Lapidarist use any other Stone/Material other than A Gemstone?

The answer to this question depends on the following:

The Value you want to get from your Work

You can choose to shape precious materials like diamonds or emeralds or synthetic ones like glass.

For practice, you could start with synthetic materials, but to perfect your skill and, at the same time, get value for your work, then you should invest in precious/semiprecious stones.

You have all the information and tips to get started, but is that all it takes to become a lapidarist?

Let's find out in this final chapter!

Chapter 8: What it Takes to be a Lapidarist

You probably are wondering...

Do I have what it takes to bring out the hidden beauty in a stone?

Or,

Is this job worth my effort?

After uncovering the processes involved in gem-cutting and polishing, we also need to understand the qualities/qualifications of an effective lapidarist.

So, let's read on:

Qualifications of a Lapidarist

Do you require to have special training to be able to work as a lapidarist?

Here is your answer:

There are no special qualifications for being a lapidarist; anyone interested in the field can succeed. However, there are courses that one can take to enhance their skills. Some countries also require that one should be licensed to be able to work with stones.

Some of the certifications that one might want to have to perfect the art are:

- **Apprenticeship training**

You can get this training from an institution or at a lapidarist's workshop. This will help you gain the appropriate hands-on skills required to work with stones.

During an apprenticeship, you become acquainted with the techniques, tools, and equipment necessary for lapidary art. You learn not just the theory of stone-cutting but the practical aspect of it as well.

- **Gemology certification**

Gemology is the science that entails the studying of characteristics and the cutting and valuing of gemstones. It involves learning the techniques of differentiating the various types of precious and semiprecious stones, both natural and synthetic. This course also gives one the skills and knowledge necessary to value these stones while researching new types.

A lapidarist does not necessarily need to have the gemology certification. However, to be able to identify the various types of gemstones skillfully, the course is relevant.

You will likely acquire many other lapidary skills during this course, including designing, lab work, jeweler, etc.

Even with these qualifications, are there some qualities you must have to become the best lapidarist?

Personal Qualities of a Lapidarist

As a lapidarist, there are attributes that you should strive to have to be excellent in this art.

These are:

✓ **Interest And Self-Motivation**

It helps when you show interest in stones and their inner beauty to work as a lapidarist.

Lapidarists see every raw gem as a unique piece with great potential to be an excellent masterpiece. They visualize the end product in their eyes by figuring out the processes they need to follow to transform the gems into beautiful pieces.

Therefore, as a beginner to lapidary art, you ought to be curious to work with stones, follow through the process, and bring out an end product worth all your effort.

✓ Creativity

Even though you do not need a degree in art to qualify as a lapidarist, you need a creative mind. A lapidarist should be able to study the stones and see what shapes would work on what kind of stones. They should be able to produce beautiful and unique pieces that stand out.

As a beginner, all you need to do is to keep up with your determination and keep on researching new ideas. The more experience you gain, the better your creativity gets.

✓ Willingness to Learn

There is quite a lot to learn in this area, and sometimes, it may feel overwhelming. However, cultivating the desire to keep improving and learning new aspects will make you a great lapidarist.

So, how do you learn?

Here are some ideas:

- Join workshops or clubs around.

- Work with more qualified lapidarists.

- Buy study materials.

All this will help you keep up to date with the lapidary world and teach you a thing or two.

✓ Patience and Precision

Working with stones can be tedious. Some rocks are rough, and to achieve the desired results, one has to work on them for many hours. Also, you must be very precise when cutting, polishing, and shaping different stones to get the right design. Again, you've got to factor in the configuration and texture of the different types of rocks and make the proper alterations to bring out the best in them.

For these things to happen, patience and precision are essential attributes you must possess.

✓ Open-Minded

This is helpful, especially when trying different designs to see which best suits your artwork. Therefore, you must be ready to make alterations to your plans, stay up to date with the tools, equipment, and techniques of lapidary, and work with your clients/market preferences.

So, what other things should you do as a lapidarist?

Additional Tips that will help make your Lapidary Journey Smooth

The activities in a lapidarist's workshop are almost the same all over. However, a day in your work may vary depending on the goals you have set for your work.

For example, you may want to invest your time in cutting and polishing the raw gem and hand it to another team for designing and jewel-making.

Or,

You may desire to complete all the processes by yourself.

In all this, you will be required to understand what your work on a day-to-day basis will involve.

So, what are some of the things you should always do?

Here they are:

- Begin by ensuring that your work meets the necessary safety standards. Use proper protective gear for yourself and ensure everyone working with you has theirs too.

- Have the legal requirements (like licenses and work permits) put in order.

- Ensure you have the right equipment for the different processes. Do you need to buy, hire, or work in another person's workshop? If you are working as an employee, you do not need to worry about that as your employer will have provided it for you.

- Again, you will be required to find the source for your raw materials—research where you can find the stones you want, i.e., online or locally.

- If you are doing it for business, identify your potential clients and keep in touch. Update them on whichever projects you may be working on. Be ready to accommodate their preferences. Have a listening ear and be attentive to detail so you can capture every specification of their orders.

- Market your artwork through art fairs, online markets, or other retail outlets available in your location.

- Properly store, maintain and care for your raw gems, finished products, tool, and equipment. As we have seen, gemstones are rare and expensive; therefore, always keep them in safe storage. Again, you need to understand the composition of your materials to protect them from elements that may affect their quality.

- Follow the manufacturer's instructions on how to use your tools and equipment.

- Use the right tool for the right task and replace those that become worn out to avoid causing damage to your pieces. Seek help from qualified professionals or the more experienced lapidarists where need be.

- If you are unsure of a particular stone that you may be interested in, research it before you begin working on it. This will help you avoid damaging your equipment or wasting too much time on stones you did not intend to use.

- Most of all, enjoy it. Bring out the best in you and show the world what beauty lies beneath those stones!

Conclusion

It doesn't matter how many errors, repetitions, imperfections, or perfections you will make; your goal should be to keep at it, fine-tune your skill and grow to the next level as a lapidarist. Practice makes perfect, and whether you will be cutting, tumbling, cabbing, carving, or faceting, lapidary art is all worth your time. Remember, have the right tools and products, follow the right processes, and soon, people will look forward to buying your beautiful gem pieces.

PS: I'd like your feedback. If you are happy with this book, please leave a review on Amazon.

Please leave a review for this book on Amazon by visiting the page below:

https://amzn.to/2VMR5qr

---

[1]   https://www.inspiringquotes.us/author/7492-francis-alexander-durivage

[2] https://www.etymonline.com/word/lapidary

[3] https://archive.org/details/introductiontola00krau/page/1/mode/2up

[4] https://journals.openedition.org/afriques/1752

5   https://www.visualcapitalist.com/the-history-of-jade-the-emperors-stone/#:~:text=The%20Origins%20of%20Jade,became%20revered%20with%20special%20significance.

6 https://www.britannica.com/science/quartz

7https://www.gia.edu/rose-quartz-history-lore

8 https://en.wikipedia.org/wiki/Silicon_carbide

9 https://www.pinterest.com/pin/314618723949538003/

10https://polishingexpert.com/rock/how-to-use-cerium-oxide-powder-for-rock-polishing/

11   https://www.zoicpalaeotech.com/products/tin-oxide-polishing-powder?shpxid=29897568-49b0-45b4-a6bb-3b5c7a4acb28

12 https://www.ebay.com/itm/204069200494

13   https://www.nps.gov/articles/mohs-hardness-scale.htm#:~:text=A%20mineral's%20hardness%20is%20a,to%20determine%20a%20mineral's%20hardness.

14 https://www.kernowcraft.com/products/gemstone-cabochons-faceted-stones/gemstone-cabochons

15 https://www.ahsapkolsaati.com/pages/agate-stone

16 https://diamondbuzz.blog/sapphire-properties-and-characteristics/

17 https://www.jewellermagazine.com/Article/8695/A-guide-to-asterism-and-chatoyancy

[18]   https://www.printables.com/model/33532-lapidary-template-stencil-thing-for-marking-rock-s

[19]   https://www.gemsociety.org/article/lapidary-fundamentals-cabochon-cutting/

[20]   https://cabking.com/pages/how-to-cab#:~:text=Cabbing%20is%20the%20process%20of,cabbing%20is%20very%20self%2Drewarding.

[21]   https://gotcharocks.com/how-to-remove-your-stone-from-a-dop-stick-lapidary-101/

[22]   http://www.gravescompany.com/6wheeler.html

[23]   https://www.aliexpress.com/item/1005002740590369.html

[24]   https://cabking.com/pages/how-to-cab#:~:text=Cabbing%20is%20the%20process%20of,cabbing%20is%20very%20self%2Drewarding.

[25]   https://www.youtube.com/watch?v=00Nkx 20Ac

[26]   https://www.diamondpacific.com/product/4-polishing-pads/

[27]   https://www.youtube.com/watch?v=gGczSrJup2c

[28]   https://www.smls.online/making-a-cabachon

[29]   https://hitechdiamond.com/collections/lap-machines/products/all-u-need-rock-mineral-model?variant=33579646976045&aff=88

[30]   https://andy321.proboards.com/thread/62050/home-12-flat-lap?page=1&scrollTo=696547

31 https://www.homemadetools.net/best_homemade_tools_ebook?source=above_tool_label

32 https://www.proantic.com/en/display.php?id=513176

33 https://china.usc.edu/calendar/colors-universe-chinese-hardstone-carving-0

34 https://en.wikipedia.org/wiki/Hardstone_carving

35 https://www.eternaltools.com/diamond-drills

36 https://www.pinterest.com/pin/cut-design-in-metal--302093087503973100/

37 https://www.eternaltools.com/diamond-wire-hand-saw-blades

38 https://www.eternaltools.com/small-diamond-twist-drills

39 https://cuttingedgesupply.store/products/120-grit-diamond-v-wheels?variant=31898543423587

40 https://cuttingedgesupply.store/collections/diamond-burs

41 https://www.rockseeker.com/how-to-polish-stones-with-a-dremel/

42 https://www.amazon.com/dp/B075C72PGK?tag=rockseeker-lasso-20&geniuslink=true

43 https://www.eternaltools.com/diamond-polishing-paste

44   https://www.amazon.com/Toolocity-DHPSET-Diamond-Polishing-Stone/dp/B00MCL4NHG

45   https://the-maac.com/product/hardstone-cameo-pendant-brooch-filippo-tignani/

46 https://www.pinterest.com/pin/397513104585719996/

47   https://www.edwardflemingjewellery.com/blog/2019/12/3/faceted-and-cabochon-gemstones

48

https://www.pinterest.com/pin/AZKk9FS5iZNwI6zM2RtBJg2kNKzLjtg02TsPup7B0mKZelI3d8Mdz3U/

49 https://www.langantiques.com/university/facet/

50 https://www.gemsociety.org/article/best-faceting-machine/

51   https://www.gemsociety.org/article/faceting-made-easy-part-2-faceting-machines-equipment/

52   https://www.dreamstime.com/royalty-free-stock-image-gemstone-image5183776

53 https://en.m.wikipedia.org/wiki/Faceting_machine

54 https://www.gemsociety.org/article/lapidary-fundamentals-gemstone-faceting/

55 https://www.gemologyproject.com/wiki/index.php?title=Faceting